IVY STEVENS

HELP!

HOW TO LOOK AFTER A NEW BABY

Development

Temperature

Illness/Problems

Crying

Weight Sleep

Feeding Travel

Bathing

What to buy

Changing Nappies

Games

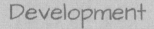

Introduction

Bringing a newborn home is one of the most magical experiences anyone can have. It is also a time of worry and panic, especially for first time parents! Most parents want to make sure that they have everything they need for their new baby before they arrive. When you have not looked after a newborn before, or it has been a while, it is almost impossible to know what they will need! Then there is the matter of how to look after them. Looking after a newborn baby is not easy. Most parents-to-be will have already had masses of information and advice from numerous different sources, including your healthcare provider, well-meaning family and friends, and strangers who spot your bump and see an opportunity to share their advice!

The aim of this book is to provide information on how to look after a newborn baby in the first 3 months of life. After the first 3 months, most parents are feeling more confident and develop their own ways of doing things, that meet their own baby's needs.

What your baby needs to survive in terms of possessions, is actually very minimal. However, most babies are showered with new clothes and gifts. Most are only worn a handful of times, if at all. If you are on a budget, there are plenty of pre-loved baby sales around, where you can buy practically new items very cheaply.

Having a baby is fantastic for bringing the whole family together. Everybody wants to come and meet the latest edition to the family as quickly as possible. This will also come with a lot of advice. The problem is, lots of the advice will be from generations ago. Some of it is useful and some of it is not. Some outdated practices amount to child abuse in this generation, such as whiskey in the bottle to help calm a crying baby!
This book will empower you, as new parents, to make your own choices on how to look after your

baby. You can then accept or reject advice from others as you please, based on your own informed decisions! One of the most controversial topics around looking after a new baby, is feeding. Most people have an idea of how they would like to feed their baby before they arrive. Sometimes, the chosen method just doesn't work out. This is because everybody, parent and baby, are different, and everyone's situation is different. Sometimes things don't work anatomically, sometimes things don't work because of work schedules. Some situations are decided by baby, who may reject one feeding method for another. Whichever feeding method you end up doing, know that the important thing is that your baby is thriving and is healthy. Do your best to ignore the opinions of others, as no matter how baby is fed, somebody will think an alternative is better!

Another difficult decision new parents have to make, is the type of car seat, and pram system to get. Most purchase this before baby arrives, and it is likely to be one of the biggest investments you make for your newborn. The benefits of different types will be discussed in the book. It is important to do your research, read lots of reviews, and try some out at the store. If you have a difficult pram or car seat, you are likely to be stuck with it for at least a year or more!

The advice given in this book is general advice, and not specific to you and your baby. It is not the intention of the author or content of the book to replace the advice of your healthcare provider. Always follow the advice of your health care provider.

What items do babies need?

What items do babies need?

The overwhelming likelihood is that you and your baby are going to end up with far more things than you could ever want, let alone use! This may seem fine to begin with, but as your child grows, you are suddenly faced with the decision of what to do with it all. A new baby outgrows clothes very rapidly. With a newborn, the most important thing to remember with clothing, is baby needs to be warm and comfortable. However, they must have layers that you can easily add, or take away to help regulate their temperature, as babies can overheat quite quickly. These layers should be easy to add and remove as this will need to be done multiple times per day. Some like to dress their newborns up in proper outfits, which are easily accessible these days, but much less practical! A newborn does not need much in the way of toys either.

Remember that baby is likely to be showered in gifts once they are here. A lot of these gifts will be items of clothing, or knitted blankets and cardigans. Before baby arrives, try to stick to getting the essentials only. If you are on a budget, you could consider writing a list of essentials, for people to get you for your baby shower.

The following are the essential items that a baby will need.

Essential Items

Clothes:
6-8 newborn short sleeve vests
6-8 newborn baby grows
6-8 bibs
6-8 muslin cloths (square cloth that is useful for anything and everything)
2-3 pairs of scratch mittens
6 x pairs of newborn socks
2 x newborn hats
A Pram suit or snowsuit - only if its winter
3 x cardigans

Bedding:

A Moses basket or carry cot

4 x Moses basket fitted sheets

6 warm blankets ideally with breathable holes

A newborn sleeping bag

Feeding:

4 x Bottles suitable for a newborn

Breast pump if you plan to express your milk

Means to sterilise bottles or breast pump

Newborn milk powder or ready-made (if required)

Travel:

A pram that will lie flat

A group 0+ car seat rear facing - suitable from
birth

A baby carrier or sling (if required)

Toys:

Black and white toy

Toys:

Rattle

Book

Soft toy

Toiletries and changing equipment:

A changing mat

60-100 x Nappies for a newborn

Barrier cream

12 x packs of baby wipes

Cotton wool balls

Nappy rash cream

100 x nappy sacks

Baby bath wash

Sponge

Plastic bath (sink works just as well)

3 x towels

A large bag to keep a change kit in

A soft hair brush

Nail clippers

Toothbrush

Toothpaste

Health:

Thermometer

Room thermometer

Bath thermometer

For Mum:

Maternity pads

Breast pads

Nipple cream

Maternity bra

Easy to prepare meals and snacks

If you are on a budget, then this may seem like a long list. However, most things can be picked up second hand quite readily, via pre-loved sales or social media. Often friends and family have old things they are willing to give away. The only thing that must be new is baby's car seat - for safety reasons.

Whether baby's clothes are new or second-hand, it is a good idea to wash them in non-biological washing powder. Most baby clothes are suitable to be tumble dried. Use a detergent that's free of colors, dyes, scents, perfumes or fragrances to help reduce the possibility of allergic reactions. A new baby's skin is delicate. Make sure that you wash all clothing before the first use, whether it's new or a hand-me-down. If the items were manufactured overseas, some countries allow chemicals, like formaldehyde, as a preservative during shipping to reduce mildew, mold and bacteria growth. It's important that the mattress pad, sheets, blankets and anything else that has direct contact with baby's skin be washed before use.

Of course, there will be the odd piece of clothing, or sweet toy, that you simply can't resist getting! These are likely to be your baby's special things, that you may cherish for years to come.

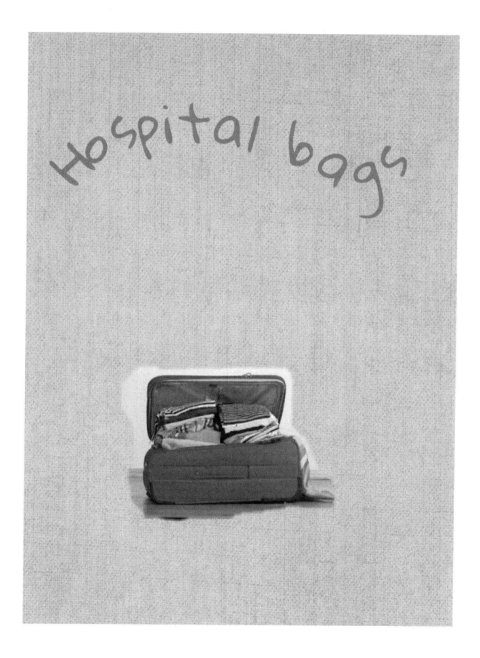

Hospital Bags

Whatever your birth plan, you must have a hospital bag packed by 36 weeks. After 36 weeks, the odds of your baby arriving are drastically increased, and you need to be prepared that you may have to go to hospital, even if you planned a home birth. This is because not all births run as smoothly as we would like. However, this is a very exciting part of preparing for a new baby. Get your birthing partner involved so that they know what you have, and where to find it!

You will need to pack two bags, one for you and one for your new baby. However, bear in mind that labour departments and hospitals do not have much space. If you have too many things, your birthing partner may end up having to take some bags home. You are just packing essentials to get you through the birth, after birth, and the journey home. If you find that you need to stay in for longer, then your partner, friend, or relative, can pop home and collect you some more items.

The last thing you will want to be doing when you go in to labour, is rushing around trying to pack your bag, so make sure this is done well in advance. Knowing what to put in a hospital bag is quite challenging! Before you know it, you have packed as if you are going away for two weeks in the sun. The following is the essentials that you should have packed and ready to go!

Mum's Bag:
Loose fitting nighty
10 maternity pads
Loose fitting nickers
Maternity bra
Shower gel
Shampoo/conditioner
Hairbrush, toothbrush and toothpaste
Dressing gown
Slippers
An outfit to go home in - loose fitting

Nipple cream

Breast pads

Energy drink/energy bars

TENS machine if you plan to use one

Your maternity paperwork

Baby's Bag:

10 newborn nappies

Barrier cream

Nappy rash cream

Wipes

Cotton wool balls

2 short sleeve vests

2 sleep-suits or baby-grows

2 bibs and 2 Muslins

A hat

Scratch mittens

Cardigan

A going home outfit - for the piccies!

2 blankets

Car seat

You may find that you can think of an odd essential more, personal to you, that you would like to take. Your birthing partner may also wish to take the odd couple of things, but they do not need to. Perhaps they could be responsible for making sure a camera is charged and ready to go. You will not be kept in hospital for any longer than you need to be, and most people are discharged home within the same day of having their baby.

Car Seats

Choosing a car seat is not quite as easy as parent preference. There are laws determining which car seats you must use for your child. These laws are in relation to the height and weight of a child. Different countries have different laws regarding which seat can be used, and how long it should be used for.

In the United Kingdom, all children must be in an appropriately sized car seat until they are 135cm (4ft 5in) tall or 12 years old, whichever comes first. Children taller than 135cm or over the age of 12 must then wear a seatbelt. In some other European countries, children must be in a car seat until they are 150cm tall, such as France and Germany. USA car seat laws differ per state.

The different rules and regulations can make it confusing for parents. The first thing you need to do is look up the law in your area, which is easily accessible on the internet. If you do not have access to the internet, you can ask in local shops that sell car seats, or ask your health care provider for advice. Luckily, the work is done for you, and if you go to a retailer that sells car seats, they will be able to tell you exactly which one you need, and how long for. However, some people like to shop around online before visiting the store.

When browsing online, it's useful to know that car seat group numbers will also be listed alongside the overall car seat category. This may sound confusing, but if you know the age, weight and/or height of your child, it is fairly straightforward.

You may see the phrase 'i-size' next to some of the car seats. These car seats are within the new parameters which are based on height rather than weight.

Eventually, all car seats will be based on the i-size system within Europe.

An example of the car seat group numbers according to weight are:

Group 0: 0-10kg (approx. birth to 6-9 months)

Group 0+: 0 - 13kg (approx. birth to 12-15 months)

Group 1: 9-18 kg (approx. 9 months to 4 years)

Group 2: 15 - 25 kg (approx. 4 – 6 years)

Group 3: 22 - 36 kg (approx. 6 – 12 years)

The weight system for grouping car seats still exists currently, and you can purchase your car seat using the above grouping method for your baby's weight. However, it is likely to be phased out in the not-too-distant future. This is because studies have shown that it is actually a child's height, and not their weight, that determines whether they are safe in their car seat or need to be moved up into the next one.

If using an i-size car seat, your child will be required to be moved into the next car seat up when they exceed the height limit for the seat. The i-size car seats have greater side impact protection under new laws. They also make it mandatory for baby to be rear facing until they are 15months old. The i-size car seats are all secured using an isofix system, whereas previous generation car seats can be fixed (in some cases) with a seat belt.

Rear-facing?

Baby's should be rear-facing in a vehicle until they are at least 15 months old. This has been shown to be much safer and can offer your child 75% more protection if you are involved in an accident. Many parents are now opting for car seats that are rear-facing until their child is 4 years old.

Isofix

This is an international standard for attachments for child safety seats in passenger cars. They can be known as LATCH or LUAS in The US or Canada.

Most cars will have ISOFIX car seat attachment points as standard. Some older cars may not have these attachment points.

If your car has ISOFIX attachment points, then you are able to purchase a car seat with an ISOFIX base or tethering mechanism.

Car seats using the older weight-based system either come with ISOFIX to install the car seat, or some can be installed using just the cars seat belt. If you are using a car seat under the new i-size regulations, then these car seats all come with ISOFIX bases. Please be warned that the ISOFIX base is often charged separately to the actual seat.

Where to position the car seat

The safest place for the car seat to be positioned, is rear-facing in the back seat behind the front passenger seat. You can get mirrors that can be fixed to the rear headrest, to enable you to keep an eye on baby in your rear-view mirror. The next safest place is the other rear seat, behind the driver, followed by the front passenger seat. If baby sits in the front, the air bag MUST be disabled.

Travel System

Some infant car seats, including a few i-size seats, can come as part of a travel system. This means that the car seat can be attached to the frame of the pram using special adapters. Some car seats attach to multiple frames with special manufacturer specific adapters. You will need to do some research online, or ask in store, if you wish for the car seat to attach to the pram, to see if it is compatible.

Safety

It is illegal to sell a car seat in your country unless it meets your countries specific safety requirements.

However, some independent companies offer additional safety and impact testing on top of the basic regulations. You can find this data online and it may guide you in choosing your car seat.

Compatibility

The car seat that you choose must be compatible with your vehicle, and must be fitted correctly, following manufacturers guidelines. You can ask the shop assistant to help you to fit it to make sure that it fits securely prior to purchase. There are many videos and tutorials online to show you how to correctly fit the car seat.

Choosing a car seat takes some research, and thought, about what will best suit you and your lifestyle. Make sure you set aside some time to research it thoroughly in order to make the right decision for you.

It is recommended that newborns are only in the

car seat for short distances, and babies for no longer than 2 hours at a time.

Car seats should be for single child use and discarded when no longer in use. It is not recommended that you purchase car seats second hand, you will not know if they have been in an accident, or dropped. Some damage is not visible to the naked eye, but could be catastrophic in an accident. Your baby's safety it paramount.

It is worthwhile to consider purchasing sun shades for your vehicle, as baby can get hot very quickly in direct sunlight.

Pram/Travel System

Choosing your pram, or travel system, is a big decision. You want one that meets all your functional and style needs. However, one thing you may not be aware of, is not all pushchairs are suitable from birth.

The pushchair should come with a lie flat option, or option to switch to a carry cot. It should indicate that it is suitable from birth on it. Babies should be around 6 months old before they can use the push chair seat in the upright position.

Once you have your pushchair and you are using it daily, there will undoubtedly be things that annoy you about it, that you wish you had thought of before purchase. Therefore, do your research before purchase, read lots of reviews to make sure that you know the niggles of others.

Some people find a travel system suits their needs. The pushchair frame is used between the carry cot, pushchair seat, and perhaps the car seat. You can easily switch between each using adapters. Others like to have the pushchair separate to the car seat, and the car seat remains in the car at all times. Either of these options are fine.

There are some things to consider:

Weight

You are likely to have to fold the pushchair and lift it in and out of the car, or onto public transport, sometimes numerous times a day. If this sounds like it could be you, you may want to go for a lighter frame. If lots of reviews suggest it's very heavy, it may not be the one for you.

Size

Think about where you will be storing your pushchair. If it needs to go into the car boot, make sure that it will fit in prior to purchase. It can be awkward to manage a pushchair that will not fit in the car!

Maneuverability

You may want to check how well the pushchair manages getting up and down pavements, and uneven surfaces including stones. If you do a lot of dog walking and uneven terrain, you may need to consider a pushchair with bigger wheels.

Reversible Seat

Some pushchairs have a reversible seat, so that baby can face you when they are newborn, and turn to face the world when they are a bit bigger. This is useful as you are likely to want to keep an eye on baby to begin with, and baby may feel scared if you are out of sight.

Adjustable Handles

If you and your partner are different heights, or you are not an average height, an adjustable handle height option may be worth exploring. A stooped posture when pushing the pushchair can lead to long term back problems, so it is important to make sure everyone that is using it regularly, will be able to do so comfortably.

Basket Size

If you like to carry around a lot of items, or will likely be doing a bit of food shopping with your pushchair, a bigger basket size may suit you better. Some of the pushchair baskets are deceptively spacious, holding three to four large bags of shopping.

Brakes

Have a good look at the brake system and try it out. The brakes should be easy to take on and off, not cause you discomfort, and work effectively. Some pushchair brakes have a habit of jumping out of place, which can be dangerous. They can also hurt your toes to put on and off or scrape your shoes.

Consider previous models

Previous models of pushchair are normally very similar in what they offer, at a fraction of the price!

Try it out

You must try your pushchair out before you purchase. Make sure that it is a comfortable height, and that you can walk at a comfortable speed and don't catch your shins or feet on any bars. Make sure the folding mechanism is efficient, and the brakes work well. Try out the buckle system. Make sure you put it in and out of your car boot, and can lift it up comfortably.

Buy now and collect later

Most stores give the option to reserve for pick up at a later date so that you don't have a pushchair in your house for months before baby's arrival!

Double buggy

If you are planning to have another child soon after the first, it is likely that you will need to consider a double buggy system.

It is very easy to pick a pushchair based on the look and style. However, it is worth the time and effort to properly research and think about which will suit your needs the most.

Birth Plan

Most people like to write a birth plan, and your midwife or healthcare provider should encourage you to do so. Writing a birth plan not only allows you to really think about the different options available for the birth of your baby, it also guides the healthcare professionals in making decisions that you would have wanted, at a time where you may not be able to make reasonable decisions. The birth plan you make is your wishes providing all progresses well with your labour. It is by no means set in stone, and very often changes if clinical need dictates it. This may be if either yourself or the baby are struggling, and need extra monitoring, or intervention. Some people find that the pain is too unbearable. Everybody's perception of pain is different, and so trying to predict what pain relief you would want in advance, can be a difficult thing to do.

When you are writing your birth plan, you need to take into account the setting that you are having your baby. If all is going well with no complications, you may choose a home birth or a birthing centre to have your baby. If this is the case, you will need to check with your healthcare provider regarding what pain relief and other modalities may be available to you at the different settings.

What to include?

Setting

You need to decide if you would like to give birth at home, at a birth centre, or at hospital. If there are any complications during your pregnancy, you may need to choose the hospital setting. However, if your pregnancy is progressing well, one of the other option may better suit your needs.

Birth Partner

Write the name and contact details of your birth partner. Try to pick someone who is reliable and who will be able to get to you when you go in to labour, even if this means in the middle of the night, or leaving work early.

Positions

Would you like to stay mobile, or rather be still with pillows. Do you want to be on all fours? Are there any positions that cause you pain? Do you have any restrictions in your exercise tolerance?

Pain Relief

You will need to find out from your healthcare provider about which pain relief options are available where. You may want to try breathing techniques, meditation, warm water, massage or TENS. You may wish to have use of gas and air or the option for an epidural.

Birth Pool

You may want to request use of a birth pool

Equipment

You may wish to use other equipment or tools, such as music, or a gym ball to help you through the birth.

Placenta

You will be offered an injection to speed up the delivery of the placenta as standard. However, you can decline this if you wish to give birth to the placenta naturally.

Straight after birth

Do you want baby cleaned up a bit, or placed straight onto you for skin to skin contact? Do you want your partner to cut the cord?

If you have any special needs then put these on the birth plan. Also, make it clear that you are happy for the plan to change if it is medically indicated. Try and discuss your birth plan with your healthcare provider before 36 weeks.

Even if you are booked in for a Caesarean section, there will still be options and preferences for you to document on your birth plan. Liaise with your healthcare provider for details of what these could be in your area.

Bringing baby home

If you chose to give birth at the hospital or birthing centre, then the moment you are discharged from hospital is often a very daunting time. You have the adrenaline and excitement of getting your new baby home, mixed with the fatigue of labour, and fear of what's to come!

Many people will be travelling home by car. You will need to have sent your birth partner to the car to bring the car seat into the hospital or birth centre, when you are ready to leave! Make sure that you have practiced the fitting of your car seat a few times before taking your new baby home for the first time. The last thing that you want to be doing is sitting in the hospital car park, with your new baby and a car seat manual, trying the figure out how it fits in properly! You are unlikely to be able to drive yourself.

Your baby needs to be dressed appropriately for the journey home. They will need a hat, a vest, and a going home outfit with a cardigan! You must not, tempting though it may be, dress your baby in a thick coat or pram suit while in their car seat. This will make the car seat ineffective, as the straps will not be tight enough. Instead, put your baby in the seat and then cover with blankets. Baby needs to be warm but not too hot. Babies find it difficult to regulate their own temperature. Check their temperature using the back of your fingers on baby's chest. If they feel too warm, remove a blanket layer.

When handling baby, you must support their head and neck at all times. You will soon feel confident in doing this! Before you know it, you are home, staring in wonder at the bundle of joy in their car seat, wondering what's to come next! This is usually the time that people are bombarded with visitors. Try and keep visitors to a minimum, this is a really important time for you and baby to bond, and rest.

Feeding

Feeding

Feeding is often a controversial topic of conversation. This is where you may get people who are very strongly opinionated one way or another. Research suggests that breast-feeding may be more beneficial for infants than formula-feeding. Breast-feeding has been shown to help protect against sudden infant death syndrome, reducing its occurrence by up to 36%. It can also protect against necrotising enterocolitis, a deadly condition of the gut. There are small benefits in reducing the risk of asthma. Breast-feeding can protect against certain infections such as diarrhoea, dental problems, chest infections and glue ear. It can also protect babies in later life against obesity and type 2 diabetes.

However, some people cannot breast-feed, and others prefer not to. Whether you decide to breast feed, or bottle feed, or a mixture of both, here are a few things to consider.

Breast-Feeding

Breast feeding is not easy, and doesn't always come naturally. You will have heard the words "good latch" while talking about breast feeding with your health provider. You must not underestimate the importance of this. Baby needs to have a good latch to gain a sufficient amount of milk at their feed before they drop off to sleep. Some babies comfort suck, they stay latched on, but are not really feeding, and your nipples will become raw. A baby should have gained all the milk they can fit in their tiny tummies within half an hour. Any longer and it is likely you have a comfort sucker. If this is the case, you may need to break the suction with your finger, and apply lots of nipple cream. Take good care of your nipples, without them you cannot feed your baby!

Your newborn will need to feed around every 2 hours. You do not need to wake your baby to feed, they will wake naturally. If you can, sleep while they sleep and try not to be tempted to stay up all night watching them! Everyone does it, but you will pay for it, and you will be much more use to baby if you are well rested.

You may need to play around with different holds to feed your baby in. Not all holds suit every baby and breast! Some prefer a traditional cross body hold, while others need to go for an under-the-arm football style hold!

The first few feeds provide baby with important fatty milk. It is important to offer baby both breasts at every feed, and alternate which breast is offered first. After 2-3 days your milk supply will 'come in' and your breasts will feel enormous. Baby is skilled at establishing a supply that meets their needs. You will know that baby is taking in enough if they are putting on weight appropriately, and having wet nappies. Be aware, that if baby is becoming more jaundiced, this could be a sign they are not taking in enough milk. Jaundice is caused by the build-up of bilirubin in the blood. Bilirubin is a yellow substance produced when red blood cells are broken down. Jaundice is common in newborns because babies have a high level of red blood cells in their blood, which are broken down and replaced frequently. The liver in newborn babies is also not fully developed, so it's less effective at removing the bilirubin from the blood. By the time a baby is about two weeks old, their liver is more effective at processing bilirubin, so jaundice often corrects itself by this age without causing any harm. Adequate amounts of breast milk increase a baby's bowel movements, which help secrete the buildup of bilirubin. Breastfeeding jaundice can occur when a newborn does not get a good start on breastfeeding, has an improper latch, or is supplemented with other substitutes which interfere with breastfeeding. Breastfeeding jaundice often will resolve itself with increased feedings and help from a lactation consultant to make sure the baby is taking in adequate amounts.

Some breast-feeding mothers suffer with blocked milk ducts. This can be painful and lead to mastitis. Baby should be content after feeds and your nipple will look as it did prior to the feed. It will not be pinched, distorted or have changed colour. You will have noticed baby start with a few quick sucks, and then settle into a long rhythmic sucking action with occasional pauses. You will have heard baby swallow. If you suspect that baby is not feeding properly, don't be embarrassed to ask for help from your health care provider. They are specialists, so can help you to figure out what it going wrong and fix it quickly.

Some mothers use breast pumps to help them to express milk, in order to allow others to feed baby overnight, or to feed baby while out and about by bottle. You may also express if your breasts are uncomfortably full, or you want to increase your milk supply. It is not advised that you introduce the bottle for the first 4 weeks of life, while your milk supply is developing. Also, the change in sucking action between bottle and breast can confuse baby, and lead to nipple rejection and termination of breast-feeding. You can buy special teats to mimic breast-feeding action. You must make sure the breast pump and milk bottle are sterilised before use following the manufacturer's instructions. You can also express milk by hand straight into a sterilised bottle.

You can store breast milk in a sterilised container or in special breast milk storage bags- in the fridge for up to five days, for two weeks in the ice compartment of a fridge or for up to six months in a freezer. Breast milk that's been cooled in the fridge can be carried in a cool bag with ice packs for up to 24 hours. Once defrosted, the milk should be used immediately or discarded. You should never re-freeze the milk once it has thawed.

Combination Feeding

When considering combination feeding, this can often suit lifestyle needs better than exclusive breastfeeding. This is where the mother continues to breast-feed but supplements this with intermittent formula feeds. Often, returning to work is a major driver for introducing a mixed feeding schedule. You must consider that introducing formula can have a negative impact on breast-feeding. It can lead to difficulties with milk supply, nipple rejection, confusion with sucking action, and termination of breast-feeding. It could be possible to try expressing milk as an alternative. It is usually advised to wait until baby is out of the newborn stage to introduce a combination feeding schedule.

Formula Feeding

For some, formula feeding is the way for them and their baby. This may be because breast-feeding has failed. It may be to allow the mother to carry on taking medication important to her health. It may be personal preference and to allow sharing of responsibility of feeding. It may help with knowing exactly how much milk your baby has taken, or allow you to free up some time to look after other children, or return to work. Some people just can't imagine breast-feeding and are against the idea from the start. Sometimes breast-feeding can add to stress and anxiety, which can already be heightened after birth. It can be frustrating at times when you feel that you need to explain why you are formula feeding. Remember that this is your baby, and you are doing what is best for them and you.

If you are formula-feeding, check instructions on the formula you have chosen. Make the formula up, as per the instructions, each time. Throw away any milk that is not used. Make sure the formula you choose meets baby's age range, and that the bottles/teats you use are suitable for newborns. You must have a means of sterilising the bottles between feeds. You must check the milk has cooled prior to giving it to baby. Try giving your baby 60-70mls of milk per feed. Again, they will need feeding at 2 hourly intervals to begin with. However, please do not become concerned if they don't take it all every time. If you were breast-feeding, then you would not know how much your baby had taken. Baby will take as much milk as they need. As long as they are gaining weight appropriately, they are fine.

<u>Wind</u>

After each feed, baby needs to burp. If they do not burp, they will experience painful trapped wind, and become extremely grizzly.
Wind your baby in a forward lean motion by rubbing and patting their back, after each feed. You will need to support their head and neck as you do. Be prepared for a small amount of milky spit up - with muslin cloths!

Cluster-Feeding

Some babies cluster-feed, especially in the first few weeks. So be prepared to be glued to your baby for a few hours. Baby's need to feed on their demand, not to a schedule. Cluster feeding is most common in the evening, although may differ between babies. This can be challenging and stressful for parents. It is very common in young babies, however, some parents notice cluster feeding returns with older babies who are approaching a growth spurt or developmental leap.

The most important thing, whichever feeding method you are using, is that your baby is healthy and gaining weight appropriately. If you have any concerns, make sure you write them all down and ask your health care provider.

Changing

Nappies

Changing Nappies

How do I change a nappy? This seems like an easy task in theory! In practice, babies are tiny, wriggly and they do not help at all! They may also be screaming from start to finish! And they are loud! The good news is, there is only usually a small amount in the nappy, and the poop doesn't smell too bad, as a newborn!

Some nappies have an indicator strip, so you know when baby has peed. The strip will change colour. When baby is ready for a nappy change, the ideal place to change them is on a change mat on the floor. This is so if baby was to wriggle or roll, they are unable to fall. Never leave a baby unattended while changing them on a surface above the ground level. Even if they have never rolled or travelled before, they can easily do so when you have your back turned.

Remove the tabs at the front of the nappy. Pull the front away and fold it over the back part of the nappy, while holding baby's legs in the air with the other hand. Fully wipe babies bottom clean, make sure you have done all creases. Always wipe from front to back, especially with girls. This is to prevent introducing bacteria from the bottom to the urethra.

Next add barrier cream to prevent babies bottom getting sore or nappy rash.

Now bag the old nappy up by rolling away from you, doing the tabs up around it and putting it into a nappy sack.

Put the new nappy on. Flatten the nappy out and pull out the two sticky tabs. These sticky tabs are on the back of the nappy. Lift baby's bottom up by the legs and insert the nappy flat underneath them to about waist height. Put baby down onto the nappy and pull the front section up on to baby's tummy. Tighten, and stick the tabs from the back of the nappy on to the front of the nappy on baby's tummy. Wash your hands thoroughly.

Dispose of the used nappy. Now you are ready to go!

For the first two days after birth, you may only get 2-3 wet nappies. However, from here, nappies become increasingly wet and heavy. From day 5 onwards, you can expect at least 6 wet heavy nappies per day.

The first few poops will be black - meconium. Meconium is composed of materials ingested during the time that baby spends in the uterus. Over the next few days it gradually changes colour to a bright yellow mustard coloured poop, which may be loose and grainy in appearance, and should be approximately the size of a large coin. Not all babies poop every day, so you will need to get used to what is normally for your baby.

Sleep

Sleep

You will have heard people say, "sleep when baby sleeps". It really is some great advice. But it's not always that easy. Some people struggle to sleep for short periods at a time, or become so overtired that you just can't fall to sleep at all. One thing is guaranteed, you will be sleep deprived during the first few weeks of baby's life and beyond.

Babies need a lot of sleep! 16-20 hours per day in fact. With all that sleep you might be thinking, great! Lots of time to rest, do the housework and get out and about. Well, you need to take into account that baby will wake to feed every 2-3 hours. So, you will, unavoidably, be sleep deprived.

The good news is that newborns are typically very good at falling to sleep. They normally just need a bit of a rock and a walk around, and off they go.

This is a job that could be given to your partner or visitors, to give you a bit of a break.

The most important thing about a newborns sleep is keeping them safe. As they are so small, and struggle to move themselves, they can suffocate if their airway becomes covered.

Babies should be put to sleep on their backs, on a flat comfortable surface, that is free from unnecessary loose material, and where the mattress reaches the edge with no gap. Babies normally start off in a carry cot or Moses basket. This is because babies have been shown to feel more safe and secure with a smaller sleeping environment. Babies may become more unsettled if placed in a large cot.

Baby can sleep in a short-sleeved vest, sleep suit and a cellular blanket or two. The room temperature should be around 18C or 64.4F. You may prefer to use a baby sleeping bag rather than blankets.

Babies should sleep in the same room as their mother or primary carer for the first 6 months. However, it is not advisable to co-sleep. This increases the likelihood of baby suffocating. Ideally the Moses basket or carry cot is kept next to your bed. At 6 months baby can move to their own room. And you can regain a small sense of freedom back!

During the first 6 months of life, babies are at a slight increased risk of sudden infant death syndrome. Also known as 'cot death,' as it usually occurs while baby is sleeping. Although the risk is very small, and experts are not entirely certain of the causes, there are certain things you can do to minimise the risks further. Do not smoke during pregnancy, or after birth. Baby should be put to sleep on their back. Make sure there is no loose bedding, or anything that baby could suffocate on. Remember newborns cannot maneuver themselves well, so may not be able to move to freedom if they cannot breathe. Do not co-sleep, especially on a sofa. Keep baby's room at the optimum temperature with sufficient bedding to maintain their temperature without overheating.

Some people like to set baby in a sleep routine when they are very little, with the hope that this carries over as they grow. This often includes a bath, bed time story, and putting baby down to sleep awake. The theory is that this encourages baby to feel confident in falling asleep on their own. As baby gets older, they are then more likely to fall asleep on their own more quickly. This works well for some, and not so well for others. For many parents, it is a case of trial and error, to see what works best for them. That might mean different approaches at different stages of development.

Generally, in the newborn phase, a baby needs to be warm, loved and well fed. They certainly should not be left to cry it out in bed at this age.

Crying

Crying

Babies cry to tell us they need something. It is their only way of communicating their needs, and they can cry a lot! Over time, you will get quicker at spotting what your baby needs. Babies respond better when they are attended to quickly. Once they are worked up, it can be difficult to calm them. Some babies need to be held all of the time, and when this is the case, parents find it easier to use slings or baby carriers, so they can still do other things. Here is a list of things to try to soothe your baby's crying!

1) Are they hungry? Babies only have a tiny stomach, which empties quickly, so feel hungry again quite quickly after the last feed.

2) Are they tired? Babies need up to 20 hours of sleep a day, so if they are not feeding, they are probably tired!

3) Do they need their nappy changing? Babies do not like having a wet or poopy nappy so will cry to tell you so!

4) Are they too hot or too cold? Feel baby's skin on their chest. If it feels too hot, remove a layer, if it feels too cold, add a layer.

5) They may be overstimulated with too much noise, touch or people. Try taking them to a quiet place for a few minutes.

6) They may want cuddles. Babies like to feel safe and secure, and enjoy cuddles particularly with mum and dad, with skin to skin contact.

7) Baby may have trapped wind. Babies struggle to remove wind themselves, and trapped wind is excruciatingly painful. Make sure that your baby is properly winded so they are not suffering.

When you are satisfied that you have been

through all the above, there are also plenty of other things to try to soothe baby's crying. Try a warm bath, which seems to work miracles for a crying baby. A walk in the pram. Some rhythmic bouncing or jigging. Holding your baby close so they can feel your breathing. A trip out in the car is always a good last resort. Some people swear by white noise, or playing the sound of a heartbeat.

Most importantly if you suspect something is wrong with your baby, they are inconsolable or unusually quiet, then trust your instincts and seek urgent advice from your medical provider.

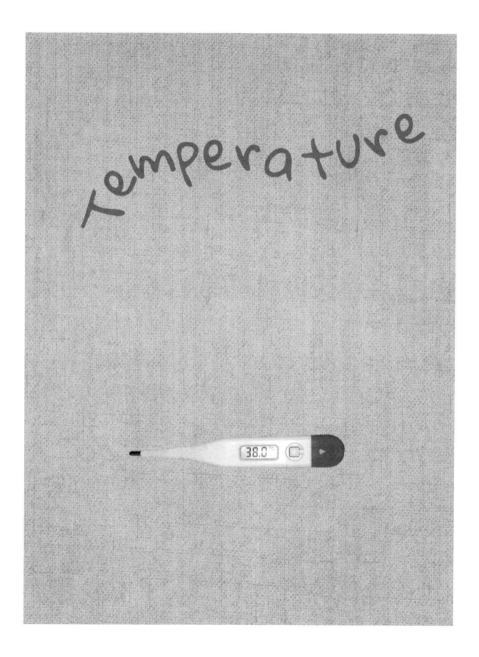

Temperature

Babies find it difficult to regulate their temperature. So, we need to make sure the environment is kept at a steady temperature for them.

Babies normal temperature will be between 36.4C-37C or 97.5-98.6F. They are considered to have a temperature if it rises to 38C or 100.4F. In the first 8 weeks of life, call your health care provider if your baby has a temperature.

The room temperature should be kept between 16-20C or 60.8-68F. If the room is this temperature then baby will only require light clothing and bedding, and you reduce the risk of baby overheating.

Your babies bath water must be at about body temperature. 37C or 98.6F is ideal and should be maintained. You can buy bath thermometers in most stores.

Weight

Weight

Babies come in a wide spectrum of birth weights. Most babies are between 5lb 6oz and 9lb at full term birth. If baby is particularly small or large at birth, they may require some extra attention from your medical provider. In most instances, they are still perfectly healthy.

Most babies will drop 7-10% of their birth weight in the first week, but most make this up by 2 weeks of age. This is normally as baby loses retained fluid. After this, babies weight should increase steadily and will be plotted on a chart to ensure they are growing as expected. Normally babies gain around 1oz per day in the newborn stages.

You will notice your baby growing very quickly, suddenly outgrowing their little outfits! Your health provider will monitor baby's weight very closely and will intervene if they feel baby is not gaining weight appropriately. Weight will be plotted on a

world health organisation growth chart, appropriate to baby's sex and age.

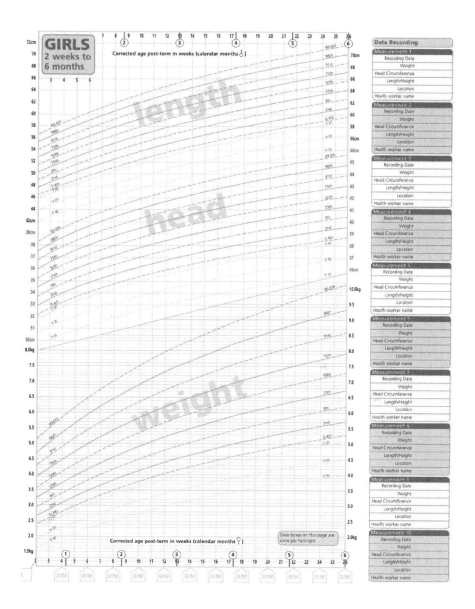

Premature babies will require extra monitoring of their weight, especially in the initial few weeks and months after birth.

After your home visits finish, your health care provider should provide you with a timetable of drop-in clinics, which you can attend in order to get baby weighed regularly. How often you attend is up to you. If there are any concerns regarding weight gain, your health care provider will let you know how often to attend.

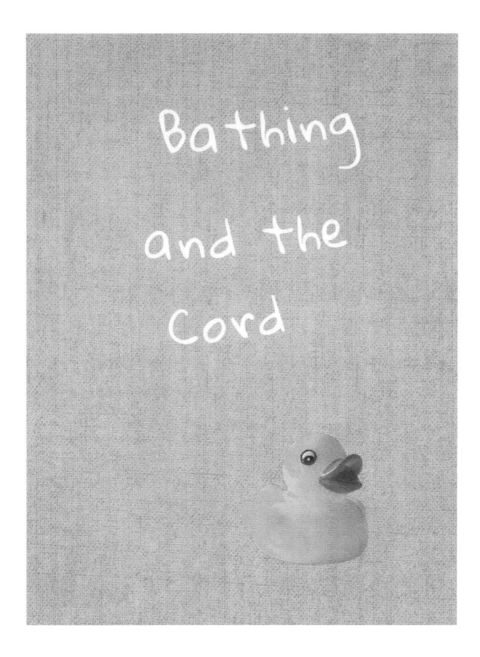

Bathing
and the
Cord

Bathing and the cord

Your baby will come home with the umbilical cord stump attached. It usually takes up to two weeks for this to dry up and fall off. Until the cord has fallen off, you need to keep it dry. Therefore, do not put baby in the bath. If the base of the cord begins to look swollen, inflamed, has a smell, discharge or pus, or is warm to the touch, seek advice immediately, as there may be an infection. In the first few weeks, clean baby's bottom thoroughly during nappy changes. Otherwise you can wipe baby down with a cloth and warm water. Ensure you do the creases such as armpits, and in the neck folds. Hands can also get sweaty quickly and need a regular wipe!

After the stump falls off, baby can be bathed in water that is body temperature 37C/98.6F. Always check the water with your hand as well as the thermometer in case the thermometer is not working properly. You can use baby bath in the water, which is enough for baby's skin. Get baby used to having their head and hair washed as soon as you start bathing them. Baby will need to be supported in the bath at all times, and of course, never left unattended.

Visitors

Visitors

Most people are immediately bombarded with swarms of visitors, who want to come and see you and baby, and want to offer every piece of advice from their experiences. While this is a lovely time for you and your family and friends, to bond and reminisce, you and baby are also in a very important stage. You will be getting to know each other, bonding, learning feeding cues and baby will be getting to know your smell and your warmth. So, if baby is being passed from person to person for the first few weeks, they are missing out on crucial bonding time with you.

You will also be exhausted. You may not have slept for a long time. Accept your visitors but put a time frame on the visit. Let them know when you are tired, or if you need to take baby away to a quiet room. Most people will understand that you need your rest and will not be offended. On the other hand, use your visitors for when you need them. If you need to sleep, you can leave them with baby for a few hours so you can have a good rest.

Common illness Problems and when to seek help

Common illness, problems, and when to seek help

Colic occurs in around 20% of babies. It can start as early as 2 weeks old. It will involve the intense crying of a baby who is otherwise healthy, sometimes for hours on end. Often it is worse in the afternoons and evenings. Baby will draw their knees to their tummy, arch their back, and clench their fists. They appear to be in pain in their tummy. Baby will grow out of this eventually, but it is important to discuss these symptoms with your health care provider to make sure that the diagnosis of colic is correct. It is very difficult to deal with a baby with colic, and it is important that you have some help to give you a break and recharge.

Most illness in babies and young children is caused by viruses. Visit your healthcare provider for a diagnosis. Your baby may develop a snotty nose, and this can cause a whole host of issues. Your baby will struggle to breath, struggle to feed, and struggle to sleep. Keep baby as decongested as you can! Stand with baby in a steamy shower room. Give baby numerous baths. You can buy decongestant over the counter suitable for babies. You can also buy little suction devices to help baby clear the snot. Remember, most viruses cannot be treated by your healthcare provider, so it is a case of riding it out and keeping baby as comfortable as you can.

Another very common problem is reflux. This is where baby brings back up a bit of milk after feeds, without vomiting. This is known as spit up. Reflux is not usually a cause for concern, providing your baby is putting on weight properly. Make sure you have your muslins at the ready! It may help baby to be slightly propped up. You can raise the head end of their Moses basket slightly while they sleep.

Nappy rash is also very common. It can cause the skin around the nappy area to become red and inflamed. It can have a rash, be scaly or blistered. The most common cause of nappy rash is from being left too long in a wet or soiled nappy. The best treatment for nappy rash is to ensure baby is thoroughly cleaned immediately after toileting. Give baby some time without the nappy on. Clean baby with water and cotton wool, and be gentle. Allow to air dry.

Most importantly, if you are worried about your newborn in any way, seek advice and support. As you get to know your baby, and they grow, you will get better and better at recognising when something is not right.

When to seek medical advice:

Trust your instincts on this. Your baby's welfare is the most important thing, and nobody is going to think you are wasting their time if it turns out to be nothing. If you suspect there is something seriously wrong with your child, then get help from your medical provider as soon as possible. Babies are very good at becoming really poorly really quickly. So, don't give it too much time to wait and see. Get help.

If your newborn develops a temperature of above 38C/100.4F, this is enough to warrant a phone call to seek help. If this is accompanied by cold hands and feet, and listlessness, seek immediate help.

If your newborn has a change in their breathing pattern, and you notice rapid breathing, panting, or noisy breathing then seek help immediately.

If baby is crying unconsolably, and nothing you normally try will console them, and the cry is not their usual cry then seek help immediately.

If baby appears floppy and you struggle to wake them, has a blue mottled appearance, seek help immediately.

If baby is choking on phlegm or vomit and you can't clear it then you call for help immediately.

You can attend a basic life support class for babies, or even complete an online tutorial. The likelihood is that it will never be used, but it may just save your baby's life if it is. Make sure it includes what to do if your baby chokes.

Most importantly, remember that this is your baby, and your instincts are usually right.

Going out
and about

Going out and about

It is important to start getting out with your baby as soon as you feel able. Start with a short walk in the fresh air, even if it's only a few yards. You can build it up gradually as the weeks go on. The fresh air will do you both some good, it's surprising how much benefit it can have on your mood and wellbeing. It is recommended that baby is pushed in a flat pram while in the newborn weeks. You have already sorted the car seat from when you brought baby home, in case you want to go a little further. It is not recommended that you take your baby on long car journeys in the newborn phase, but short trips to the shops or the park are just fine.

If it is summertime, remember that your baby should not be exposed to direct sunlight. Keep baby in the shade and use sunscreen. Remember, it can get extremely hot within the pram. It may be better to wait until the evening to go out, or go out in the early morning.

Taking a friend or partner with you for the first trip out will help with your confidence.

Baby Blues

Baby blues are very common after child birth. It is thought to occur in 8 out of 10 new mothers. It may leave you feeling grumpy, tearful, anxious and unable to sleep. You may find yourself frantically worried about your baby's wellbeing.

They are thought to be caused by big hormonal changes that occur in the week following child birth. Sleep deprivation and the mourning of the loss of your old life as you start a new journey as a mother can compound the problems.

The baby blues do not last forever, and you normally start to feel better at the end of the first week. If you still feel depressed after a month or so of giving birth, then speak to your health care provider. It is likely that you have post-natal depression. This is not uncommon, and there is plenty of help and support out there for you. It is important that you are not embarrassed or ashamed, so you can get the support you need when you need it.

Your partner can help by:

Helping you to organise your time, and prioritise jobs

Allowing you to cry

Help you to get some rest

Offer you reassurance and remind you of what a fantastic job you are doing

Clean the house

Cook dinner

Help where they can with baby

Listening to you

Try not to hide how you are feeling. This tends to make the symptoms worse, and last for a longer period of time.

Games
and
Development

Games and development

Babies are monitored at certain points in their development to make sure they are meeting developmental milestones. These milestones are what the majority of babies should be able to achieve by a certain age. Babies need full support with careful head and neck placement when they are newborn. By 3 months of age, most babies should be able to raise their head and their chest while lying on their stomach, and support their weight through their arms in this position. To achieve this milestone is an important step towards achieving other motor milestones. Baby must be given plenty of 'tummy time' to achieve this., which can begin from day 1. Start with a few minutes per day, and gradually build the time they can stay on their tummy for. Interact with them and make a game out of it. Try and make tummy time an enjoyable experience, as some babies can learn to hate it very quickly!

Baby should be able to stretch out their legs and kick, whether they are on their front or their back, and push down through their legs when they are supported on a firm surface. Baby should be able to make a fist and release with both hands, and use hands the grasp toys, swipe at dangling objects, and bring hands to mouth. You can help baby to achieve these motor skills by playing lots of games, passing them rattles and soft toys, and giving them lots of positive feedback through tone of voice and facial expressions.

By 3 months, most babies can focus on faces, and track objects across a room. They have developed a smile and enjoy play. They have some hand eye-coordination, and can recognise familiar faces, even from across a room. Baby may begin to babble, imitate sounds, and turn their head to where sound is coming from. You can encourage baby by constantly talking to them, make silly sounds and facial expressions!

Make Memories

Amongst all of the chaos, remember to make the most of every single second! Play games with your baby, talk to them and sing to them. Read them lots of stories and give millions of cuddles. Give baby daily tummy time, make silly sounds and faces! Give baby different textures to feel, and sounds to hear. Have fun, take lots of photos and make lasting memories. Your baby is not a baby for long, and the time goes by so quickly. Before you know it, they are grown and ready to leave home. This initial bond that you make together, will last a life time.

There are lots of baby journals available to document baby's first year of life and make hand and foot prints. These are fantastic to look back on as your child gets older, for all of the family.

Printed in Great Britain
by Amazon